SHAPE OF A WOMAN

By Jen Elizabeth

Table of Contents

The Things That Shape Us 3

The Broken Girl 13

The Note I Never Got 23

The Things We Don't Talk About 34

The Animal 44

The Things We Lay To Rest 57

The Things We Hold On To 68

The Call To Arms 76

Manifesto Of The Brave And Broken-Hearted 78

I Used To Try To Be Good. 80

SHAPE OF A WOMAN

"When a woman tells the truth, she is creating the possibility for more truth around her."

-Adrienne Rich

The Things That Shape Us

I believe there is a revolution happening amongst women today; a revolution in healing. A shift in the way we see our pain as a thing to be embraced rather than feared. I'm talking about a feminist movement of a different kind. I think that many of us have been fighting so hard to fit into "a man's world", that we are actually playing a part in the beautiful differences between us and our male counterparts, becoming less and less celebrated. I believe… the emphasis we have put on to looking, acting, and feeling "equal" to the men in our environments, is robbing the world of what we as women have to offer. We are tender yet powerful healers. It is ingrained in our very being to express and share emotions. I appreciate all women who follow their hearts and fight for what they believe. I honor anyone who fights for their convictions. I am so grateful for those who stand up for anyone's freedom to be their authentic selves!

We do not all have to be on the same battlefield in order to support each other's wars! The center of my being feels drawn to meet a different need. My soul feels called to glorify the very things that differ between men and women. The matters of the heart. The healing of our deepest wounds. The expression of our emotions. The distinct ways in which we navigate our way through pain. The steps we take to recover from our pasts.

How do we remain soft yet empowered?

What are the things that truly shape us? The things that affect the way our souls travel through life; the experiences that construct our sense of self and how we view the world around us. These are more abstract, personal.

How do we become broken inside?

Searching for years, sometimes our entire lives for some sort of answer to relieve us of the pain and heaviness that just builds and builds, the longer we carry these burdens?

These are the things that are much harder to define and even more difficult to put into words. Yet I think it is these very things that we absolutely must learn a language for. We have to find the courage to talk about these parts of us, the parts that hinder us and block us from abundance. They are the things that throw shade on us when we find ourselves in the sun. They keep us in abusive relationships with others and even more damaging, abusive relationships with ourselves! Addictions and disorders develop from the womb of these uncharted and unspoken territories.

How do we stop apologizing for speaking out about our pain?

I have not always felt this way. In fact, I was a believer of the exact opposite. I have essentially lived most of my life as a misogynist. Prejudice against my own gender. Pretty messed up right? Talk about being at war with yourself. It is my truth. I had very little respect for women. And I grew to hate myself for being born a female. I am not gender confused. I have never felt like I wanted to become a man. I set out to prove I was different somehow; that I was not weak, not emotional, that I could fight with best of whoever crossed my path… I was not going be a victim!

I was raised up until the age of nine in a very oppressive religious cult. When I was two and a half years old, my parents, along with other young families travelled across the country to join a growing community of other families. It was a big religious movement in the 70's. We left our extended families and friends behind in the hopes to exist in an untainted world of God fearing people. And although I believe there were beautiful intentions on the parts of my parents and the other young impressionable adults who followed, the experience there was anything but of God. I witnessed women being treated as tragically less than the "head of the household." Being taught to "obey their husbands" at any level. Men being governed by other men, once their peers turned into their shepherds. Every facet of our lives was dictated by men who allowed the power that religious leaders hold, turn them into evil dictators.

These belief systems were passed down to us, the children. The innocent children of the flock. As a little girl I was shown what good girls do to remain in God's good graces… to reserve my ticket into heaven. I was burdened with the responsibility of securing my family's membership in the church. I was the sacrifice made in the name of tithing, a payment that my dad's income wasn't capable of covering.

I felt honored in a way that only a little girl can feel.

To be chosen. To be worthy of "special" attention given to me behind closed doors. I never fought him off. I never made a stand or told anyone. And I have no memory of him ever even mentioning that I should keep our secret between us. Somehow, I just knew.

I was only 5 years old.

That experience in my very first years on this earth began to shape the way I felt about myself. The image I saw when I looked in the mirror. The way I viewed women as a whole. I did not grow up in revolt of that oppression. I did as so many of us do with our childhoods… I grew to repeat what I was shown. Joining in those demeaning behaviors against women.

I despised probably the only thing I cannot change about myself… that I was born a female. It doesn't matter what we do to our bodies; what we wear or who we have sexual relationships with. If that is your truth, that is your truth! Period.

So not only did I join in on derogatory jokes and opinions of my women-bashing male friends, I absorbed them. I saw the emotions of women as handicaps that kept them weak. I viewed their desires to love and be loved as targets on their head that made them victims. And therefore, I silenced and stuffed my own natural ways of feeling and interacting with people and life around me deep in pit of shame that had been growing inside of me ever since I can remember.

I could not deny my womanhood; instead I began starving her of love and acceptance. I viewed myself as worthless and I treated myself accordingly. I was dying on the inside. Suffocating. Drowning in shame. But on the outside, I acted tough. I was in constant competition with myself to prove that I wasn't weak. To show anyone around me that I was anything but vulnerable. I put myself in dangerous situations over and over again to prove that I couldn't be broken.

But oh my God... was I fucking breaking!

So where do we begin? Where did I begin?

Are we born with this gnawing ache to abandon our true selves? Or do we learn it along the way? Are we teaching our daughters to bow their heads and shuffle through this life in an attempt to keep them safe from harm? In hopes of protecting them from standing alone amongst the wolves? To spare them of feelings; of any feelings at all? Are we robbing them, ourselves, and this entire wounded world of the very gifts that we as women are given by God, the universe or whatever higher power you believe in, has bestowed upon us? And why?

What about the relationships with our mothers? They are the first and most influential woman figures in our lives. We are nurtured and grown from them. We get into their makeup and hair curlers, trying to emulate the ways of a woman. Their ways of womanhood. We learn how to be women ourselves by watching the way they carry themselves.

The ways in which they love themselves teaches us how to love ourselves.

The ways in which they hate themselves teaches us how to hate who we are as well.

Yet, there is not enough literature about this crucial bond between mothers and their daughters. I have found tons about fatherless daughters. The "daddy syndromes" of women who grew up without dads or poor examples of them. Daddy's girls. A daughter's first love. Dad and daughter dances. Marrying men like our fathers. But what if we grow up to become women like our mothers? Is who we are, not more important than who we date? It is a terrible injustice to women, by women, to concern ourselves so incredibly with who we date and who we will marry; over who we see when we walk past a mirror.

And what if our mothers are mentally ill? If the very women we are first introduced to, first try to befriend, the women who are given the amazing gift and responsibility to nurture us, are unable to do so appropriately? What if they are too sick to properly love us and teach us how to love ourselves? Children born of mentally ill mothers are taught to tip toe through a very unstable world. And we are groomed to be secret keepers. To keep that instability and madness protected for fear of somehow dishonoring our mothers; bringing shame to our families. We are burdened with the impossible responsibility of not making them sad or angry.

We begin to lose the child within us.

So we stuff it. We hold it in. We do our best to digest it and make sense of events and experiences that we are simply too young to comprehend. We lay in our beds at night coming up with our own theories and explanations for why things are the way they are in our homes. For why mommy is sad. Why mommy is screaming at us. Why won't mommy eat? What did I do to make mommy want to kill herself?

And no one fucking talks about it!

No one sits us down and tells us anything. We just carry on like it never happened. Picking up our moms from their stays in mental hospitals with the required happy smiles on our faces so as not to disrupt the peace that our dads are so desperate to have.

With mental illness, we also have the huge internal battle of knowing that this is not the faults of our moms. Mental illness is not something one chooses for themselves. My mother did not ask to be bi-polar. She isn't being punished for some past life transgressions. And she did not do anything in this life that God is punishing her for and causing her to be so unstable.

I know it is not her fault!

But out of all the realities I have come to understand in my life… of all the things I have had to come face to face with, to chew up and spit out… this is one of the most important:

It is not my fault either!

She is not my responsibility. Destroying myself in order to keep these family secrets is not my lot in life! It is not a cross that God has asked me to bear in silence. Just as she did not ask to suffer with mental health issues, I did not ask to be born into madness!

If you have ever kept your truth under lock and key for any length of time, then you will understand when I say that my untold stories grew over the years into a rabid beast that I was no longer able to contain on my own. The shame and guilt of my childhood ripped my heart into shreds. All of the things I learned about from the men of God. The ways in which my mother showed me how to abuse myself, starve myself, and blame myself for all of it… became the voices that played in a loop in my ears, so loudly, that I could not function anymore.

Until I found alcohol. And oh my God! Silence. Peace. My body wasn't ugly anymore. I didn't give a shit about what my heart hurt over. It was a miracle for a time. But alcohol slowly began to not be enough. I progressed to needing something stronger. And my life into the hell and darkness of a hopeless addict began. I ran. I ran from my past. I hid from my present and I destroyed any type of future I may have had.

It is not our stories that destroy us. It is the repression of our pain, the denying and avoiding of our truths, that hurt and eventually demolish us. There is this collective idea that if we talk about our pain, we are painting ourselves as victims. If we share the secrets that we have been taught to keep, that somehow we are placing blame on others for the paths we choose to take as adults. We are terrified of being judged. Of wearing labels like a scarlet letter on our clothing.

I will honor my pain.

And contrary to what a lot of unhealthy people will try and convince you of, you can honor your pain without dishonoring those around you! And we do not have to do this healing in the dark corners of our closets. Listen, there is no way around it… how we see ourselves sets the absolute standard for how everyone around views us as well. And what's even more devastating, is the way it shapes how our children grow to see themselves.

I have come to realize that women are such incredibly strong and nurturing creatures. I am honored to be a woman today, to be amongst women. It's time to begin nurturing ourselves. To come out of isolation and find a language for the things that shape us. To find a voice for the pain we have suppressed out of fear of being seen as a victim or as vulnerable. We must learn to hold and rock the little girls inside of us, so that we can grow into the amazing women we were born to be. Let's lay down the weight of the baggage we were never meant to carry. So we can then have the strength to pick up the pieces of ourselves that we have let fall along the way.

Where did we get this crazy idea that if we don't speak of our pain then it doesn't exist?

There is a huge difference between explaining the "whys" of your heart and making excuses for your behavior. I do not stand with enabling people to be dysfunctional. I do not agree with remaining stuck in our misery because its most comfortable. I believe in empowering and encouraging others to feel the fucking ache. To walk through the storms they have been avoiding.

If the only way *out* is *through*, then that is exactly what we need to do!

And that is exactly what I have done. And I will not be quiet and heal behind closed doors. I will tell my story… the messiness and the miracles. The beauty and the filthy beasts that lived inside of me. I will not tip toe for fear of judgement. The world will not fall apart from us setting the experiences that shaped us free!! It may, however become a house of pain if we don't!

I am not bound to how I have been shaped. There are things in my life that are absolutely inarguably my responsibility. And there are things that were never mine to carry. There is something magical that happens when we brave this world unmasked, unarmed, and ready to heal… it inspires others to let their own truths run free.

This is my journey through the fire.

I am woman….

hear me heal.

*"She did not want to move,
Or to speak.
She wanted to rest, to learn,
To dream.
She felt very tired."*

-Virginia Woolf

The Broken Girl

One thing I never say to my children is that they are bad. It doesn't matter what behavior they may be exhibiting or what words they have said. They are not bad. Shame and guilt… the difference is not something we automatically recognize. Especially as children. Guilt is feeling remorse for something we have done. Shame is feeling remorse for who we are! No child should be taught to hate themselves.

I was taught shame. The church my parents joined when I was little was governed by shame and psychological warfare. And everyone was controlled by the fear of going to hell. Whether or not you believe in a heaven and hell or karma or just simply negative consequences for the things we do in life... it is those fears that keep us in line so to speak.

I remember when I was around five years old a neighborhood girl had given me a poster of Whitney Houston as a gift. Now, mind you, this was in the 80's when she was still the innocent pop princess. Before Bobby and the crack. The harmlessness of this little poster was clear. I had the poster in a toy box in my closet where is kept all of my special stuff. I had never even listened to her music or even heard of her before. I was kept away from any music or cartoons or festivities that were not from our church. My parents found it. I was punished and shamed for idolizing a false god. I had given in to the demonic warfare that loomed all around us at all times. I had failed the devils temptations of worldly things.

I was a bad girl.

I wasn't allowed to spend time with that friend anymore.

In this church, we were constantly reminded of the devils fight for our souls. Whether I believe in that today or not is irrelevant. I choose to focus on the good in the world, the work of God in my life... versus the spiritual warfare I was taught to fear as a child.

My son gets a privilege taken away for being disobedient. The discipline fits the behavior. We talk about it. I hug him and tell him I love him and know what a good boy he is. I never want my children to feel the extreme heavy weight on their shoulders as I had placed on mine at their age.

I was going to hell.

My family would be brought to face the charges of my behaviors. Even the smallest act of disobedience or disorder carried detrimental consequences. It was terrifying. I constantly felt like a terrible person. I was a disappointment. I could never seem to live up to Gods expectations of me. Until the day I was chosen...

I was given the chance to make it "right." To be close to someone who I was taught to believe had my ticket to heaven in his hands. Not only my ticket, but my family's position in the church would be secured as well by my special relationship with this man. He touched me. He tickled me. He told me I was good. God I hated how he smelled. I felt nervous and confused. I remember giggling a lot out of fear. He said I was one of Gods special girls. And since he was so much closer to God than I was, I believed him.

Everyone believed him.

Memorizing my weekly bible verse while sitting on his lap. His hands would wander. My heart would race. Feeling him breathing on the back of my neck. I would drift off inside of my mind. Imagining I was riding a horse or eating an ice cream. I don't even know if I was actually reciting my verses.

I would leave my body to him and survive in my imagination.

To this day I don't know how many times I spent with him. But it doesn't even matter to me. What I do remember is enough.

I never fought him off. I never stood my ground. I never tried to get away, and I don't remember ever even really wanting to. I felt a sense of honor in a way to be in the presence of and part of something that had been painted to be sacred. I was special and I took pride in that.

Good girls don't cause problems. Gods children don't question authority.

And I never told anyone.

I was raised in an environment of mind control, social pressure, orchestrated deception, psychological and physical abuse by the hands of a few charismatic leaders. We left our natural families and were discouraged to have any real contact with them anymore. We all lived, ate, went to school, and associated with only other fellow members. Until one day when I was nine, all of a sudden, we moved…

We didn't say goodbye to anyone that I remember. All of these "family" members whom we had spent every waking moment with… weren't there to see us off. I never got to say good-bye to my childhood friends that I had grown up with. It was sudden. It was fast. And no one talked about it.

Many years later, I was approached to be interviewed for a documentary being made about all of our families and the movement across the country to join this cult. In those interviews I found out that a man had started coming around and secretly offering families a way out of the situation. To help them break free and return home. My dad, went against the church, against my mom, and broke free all on his own.

It was the bravest thing my dad has ever done.

And although this church was disbanded in the late 80's and early 90's as a documented cult, the effects of what happened to me there will be with me forever.

I was a secret keeper. I never had to be told to keep quiet. By anyone. About anything. Somehow I just knew that was what was expected of me. By him, by family, by God. It was the unspoken golden rule.

It was in the keeping of the secrets more than the actual secrets that I kept, that literally almost killed me.

In my mid 20's, I found myself incarcerated yet again for my ever-growing drug problems. I cannot say that jail holds much rehabilitation as whole. But in this particular sentence, the judge had denied my eligibility for any more out-patient help, due to my horrible track record of not complying with the terms I would always agree to. I was sentenced to a six-month in-custody drug treatment program. And if I could find that judge today, I would hug him so tight! Because even though it was not the end of my addiction story, the things I found out about myself while in there, changed my life!

The Broken Girl

I remember being in a group that we were all required to participate in. On this particular day, they had us watch a documentary. The camera crew was following this young lady and her mother as they made the journey to confront a family friend of the mother about sexually abusing this daughter throughout her childhood.

I can't recall everything that was said. But the visit was quick; almost pleasant. They spoke of the abuse very briefly. There was no outburst by the woman or her mother. The man made a very casual apology and then they all went on to talk of other things. They discussed the drive there, the weather, a painting he had hung in the hall. The mother hugged him goodbye. The daughter followed suit and gave him a hug as she left also.

The camera was focused in on the daughters face as the two ladies began walking back to their car. Uncomfortable silence fell over even the camera men. You could literally feel the stages of this woman shattering to pieces with each step she took.

All of the sudden she stopped in the middle of the parking lot and collapsed to her knees. Her face practically on the pavement. After a few seconds she lifted her head, her eyes meeting the lens of the camera. Her face was filled with more emotions than I can even find the words for. The pain so great, her face almost looked distorted. And she let out the deepest most primal and gut wrenching scream that I had ever heard in my entire life!

Even though my ears had never heard this sound before… I knew where this kind of cry comes from in a person.

As I was sitting there, an inmate in my little chair… staring at this worn out television set. Watching this woman whom I did not know, lose absolute control over her emotions; my entire body began shaking. A wave of nausea overcame me. My face ignited with heat. And the first tears shed for the little girl of my childhood began pouring down my cheeks.

I could not look at the screen anymore. I just listened as she raged at herself for abandoning her truth and all that she was worthy of.

And I raged with her.

It is not the truth of our stories that destroy us. It is the abandoning of our self-respect and the denying of our own pain that eats us alive. Quickly dismissing what you feel and sweeping your truth under the rug for the sake of avoiding conflict is NOT forgiveness! It will fester in your soul and grow into a beast so big that there will come a day when you can no longer contain it within you.

That was the day my truth broke free. I had no drugs or alcohol to try and silence it. I could not run. I was stuck; face to face with all the secrets I had been taught to keep.

A few days later I had a one-on-one meeting with my assigned therapist… another absolute God-sent angel of my life, and we began hacking through my wreckage. We discussed shame a lot. When a child does not tell anyone about abuse, a very disturbing event transpires over time. They begin to feel like a participant. A willing participant.

"Why was I such a perverted child?" "I must've liked it!" "I should never have children, I'm probably a pedophile myself!" "I am so disgusting." "I hate myself." These types of statements ran through my mind on a loop. Over and over and over! Repeatedly beating the little girl I was into a twisted rag doll. And the therapist said to me, "The reason children don't run home and tell mommy and daddy or any other adult in their lives, is because they don't feel they will be protected."

At 26 years old, suffering from a drug addiction that had reduced my entire life to a jail cell… It was time to call mommy and daddy.

What happened in that phone call absolutely crushed me. I told them my truth… well, as much of it as I was comfortable with. I left out any specific details. I guess maybe I still felt unsure if they were safe enough to protect my heart. Here I am a grown woman… in the fight for her life against an absolutely bottom-dwelling heroin and meth

The Broken Girl

addiction. My dad's response, "I had a feeling something like that had happened." Then he proceeded to take my pain and make it his own. He later went on to completely break my trust and the confidentiality I begged him for. I am so relieved that even to this very day, I have never disclosed the entire truth of my story to him.

My mother, she just dismissed it. She has never said she doesn't believe me. But she has never told me she does. She never says anything. That's just how she is. As long as she doesn't take a side... she can float between both to suit her need for that moment.

I am so incredibly grateful that I was safely locked away when I made that phone call.

After I got off the phone, I fell to my knees. My head almost to the cement floor. After a few seconds, I looked up and let out a scream I had only just heard once before. And right before I thought I may lose control over my emotions.... It hit me like a ton of bricks right in the chest; "She was right! My therapist was right!!!" I wasn't a sick and twisted little girl. I didn't like being touched. I wasn't asking to touch him.

Not a single second of it was mine to carry!

I did not participate by keeping the secret! Somehow in my little-girl mind, with no life experiences or knowledge about anything of the world... I knew I would not be believed. I knew I would lose control over my own safety.

And he fucking knew it too.

That phone call freed me just a little bit more from the torture I was inflicting onto myself as punishment for all the years I disowned my truth. For all the times I swallowed what I was worthy of saying.

Things happen in life that we have no control over. One of those is how people are going to receive you. And to be honest, I don't think there is a way to be fully prepared for any reaction. It's not about what you will hear. It's about what you need to say.

Here's the thing... we carry this deep burden of shame and responsibility for what happened to us when we were just children. And then we put even more guilt on top of that by somehow feeling we are now also responsible for the lives of any other children that may have come in contact with our abuser by us not feeling safe enough to speak up sooner. Or speak up at all for that matter.

How long are we expected to carry the weight of another's behavior?

The hard truth of it is this, I have abused myself far worse and for much longer than I ever even knew the "man of God." I victimized myself year after year after degrading year because I believed it was somehow a reflection of who I was.

I no longer take any responsibility for what happened to me as a little girl! I no longer carry the burden of anyone else's behaviors either! I am not responsible for any other person, man, woman or child. My being a victim as a child is my wound to heal. And no one has a right to tell me what to do to pick myself up and put myself back together. Any other way of thinking, has just lead to me abusing myself over and over again for so many years longer than I was actually abused.

It is not my fault. Period.

It is not your fault. Period. And it is your choice to do what you feel with your story. Because you own it! If you have given your abuser your entire life... today is the day to take it back! If you have been silent, today is the day to speak it into the air. Because guess what? It already exists! Whether you need to do that quietly to yourself in a mirror at first or tell a therapist; call a family member or your spouse... just get it out! Release yourself from the shackles you have been keeping yourself in!

It is not easy. But neither is living in undeserved shame and self-loathing.

There may be many bridges that you will need to cross along the way to freedom. Only you will know how to walk through your childhood. I do what I feel in my heart is right. For me.

For the little girl I left in the dark like a piece of trash.

What if I told you that the trauma you are so viciously protecting inside of you is the very thing that will set other women free? What we choose to do with our stories of our childhoods is up to us. We are no longer required to live a life owned by anyone else. But what a gift to be able to heal ourselves and at the same time make space for other women who are trapped in their pasts to feel safe in speaking their truth!

I have laid down what was never mine to carry. Which gave me the strength to then pick up the pieces of my shattered life that I am responsible for gluing back together.

My story has been told. To whom I choose to tell it. I share it freely to help other women find their own voice. And until the day I die, I am holding the pen to my own life! And the ending can be rewritten at any time.

Because its mine.

"No child comes to save her mother."

-Stephi Wagner

The Note I Never Got

Trying to bring the experiences of life with my mother out of the shadows onto on a piece of paper is very difficult. I love my mom. And even though I know in my heart of hearts that I must get my pain out… for myself and for other women who have had to cope with haunting family secrets that they have carried in every inch of their beings, it has been so ingrained in me to protect her.

At all costs.

Even at the cost of my own existence. Going back in time always leaves me on the floor in front of my mother's closed door.

My mother was so beautiful. She had thick curly dark hair and crystal blue eyes. She was given a gift of music that made her a star on several stages. There are photographs of her in her teens with music deals and awards. She can play and write music by ear, never reading a single note. I remember seeing her perform at events for our church when I was little. To me, she was a super star.

I idolized her.

I remember watching her do her makeup. I wanted to be just like her. She was petit and powerful. Beautiful but broken. Incredibly smart and sad... so sad. There's not a simple explanation for what happened to my mom. But her mental health really took a dark turn after we left the church and moved back to California.

I know that she has always battled mental health issues. Long before I was ever born. My dad says when they were dating she would lock herself in her apartment for days. Stuck in deep depressions and phases of uncontrollable mania.

My dad believed he could fix her.

I believed it was me who broke her.

Living in a home that is plagued by mental illness creates a lot of confusion for a child. You learn to tip-toe for fear that you will cause mommy to get upset. You learn a way of life that would make no sense to anyone else; so you don't say anything once you walk out the front door.

Being in my mother's light was intoxicating. When you were in her good graces it felt like you were the sun and the moon in her sky. She has a way of loving you that can make all the clouds that were just looming overhead, completely disappear.

It is no wonder that my dad fell in love with her. He chased her and she wasn't interested. She would go on these camping trips all alone to write music under the stars. I think she loved solitude. They both tell the story of the time my dad followed her up the mountain to try and convince her to go on a date with him. She finally agreed.

On their first date, they took a long walk together, where my dad picked her a flower of every color along the way. They dated for six weeks before they got engaged. And I came along a year after they were married. It would be considered a whirlwind romance in this day in age. They were twenty-one.

My mother's personality is just like that bouquet of flowers. There is one for every side of her, each with its own unique bloom. The vivid colors and smells would never leave you the same. But you never knew when you were going to break the next stem. She made promises of taking us on trips or to the beach. She would buy one thing every week to make it extra special. A beach ball. Towels. Sand toys. A sun dress and hat. But we never went.

The only places we really went, were along the rides of her mania.

To obsess on things and then just as soon as it was there, it would be gone. I can make sense of it now as an adult who has compassion for her illness and all that comes with it. But as a little girl, it was just disappointment after disappointment. And all I could come up with on my own was that I must have done something to make her sad.

So, I learned pretty young that being in the warmth of her sunlight was not a safe place to be. It was unsteady. Unsafe. Because without warning it would be taken. And her eyes would go dead; her body would stiffen.

Just nothing. No love. No more breeze blowing through her beautiful hair. No more strokes with her long fingernails on my arm. She would be gone.

I was constantly scrambling around trying to bring her back.

Our mothers are our first girlfriends. They are the ones who show us how to be soft and nurturing. They teach us how to love our bodies and feel safe inside of them. My mom wasn't able to keep herself together long enough to show me much but how to be afraid of losing her. I was left to try and make sense of things that do not make sense.

The memories I have as a kid come to me in hazy flashes. A mix of out of focus images and muffled sounds. But the feelings of my childhood... the feelings are extremely clear. Every moment I can visually recall is almost completely overshadowed by the intense emotions that accompanied them.

The pit of my stomach becomes hollow. My heart beats faster with anxiety; palms begin to sweat and a cloud of confusion fills my head.

Confusion.

Maybe it wasn't confusing at all. Perhaps I wanted experiences to be perplexing because the facts of what was in front of me was too painful to accept. Not much confuses me today. And as I take an honest look back at my life... I guess not much truly has.

I desperately did not want to understand my mother. I searched for ways to keep her puzzling; to find her a mystery. To face her behaviors head on as they were, was more damaging than to just keep myself lost in the chaos. I have known since I was very young that my mom didn't love me the way other girls moms loved them. I suppose that's where my confusion rested.

There have been many times in my childhood and up through my late teens when my mother made attempts at suicide. Followed by countless stays in hospitals. With returns back home as if nothing ever happened. There are so many pink elephants in my family, that it is difficult to even catch your fucking breath.

My mother's mental illness is one. Her regular efforts to end her life are another.

As I sit here, a woman... I am able to sift through those behaviors and clearly see that she was crying for attention. Seeking affection. Desperate to have needs met that no one could ever manage to supply her. But as a young girl, each attempt felt terrifyingly real.

Images of police cars outside my house and the look in my dad's eyes because yet again, mom is missing. The disappointment heavy on his face as, he too was confronted by the truth of her. She wasn't better. Life wasn't going on.

But he said nothing.

One particular day vividly haunts my memory. I was around 14 years old. I had just turned off my shower water and began drying off when I heard the front door shut. It was only my mom and I home at the time. Like most of the times she took off, it was either me who was left behind or me coming home and find her gone.

Not my dad. Not my brother.

Me.

I used to believe it was because she hated me. But I have come to realize it was less about hurting me. And more about not wanting to hurt them.

I ran down the stairs in my towel. Water dripping from my hair. Panicked. I cracked the front door open to see her; cane in one hand, purse over her shoulder… calmly walking down the sidewalk. I yelled for her to come back inside. Trying to stay hidden behind the small break in the doorway. Because for a young teenage girl, being half-naked is a huge cause for embarrassment.

She turned to me with a look that I will never forget. And spoke with a voice that gives me chills as I remember the sound. She told me to stop making a scene. To go back inside the house. She said she was just going for a walk. She was looking right through me as she mocked me and my panic. But my mom never went for walks. I knew.

I always knew.

I literally begged my mother to please come inside. And finally she agreed. All the while telling me I was being emotional and ridiculous. Once I knew she was safe inside I ran to the kitchen to call my dad at work. When he picked up the phone, the only words I managed to get out to him were, "Help me, mom's trying to leave us again." And I heard the front door again.

I dropped the phone, swung the front door wide open… too overcome with fear to be concerned about modesty; I ran after my mom. A strange shift happens when you are a daughter of a mentally ill mother. The roles reverse. I felt responsible for her, like a parent should feel for their child if they are about to run into the street without looking both ways.

Crying and pleading for her not to do this. "Please mom. Come inside! I love you! I need you here. To be with me!"

Begging my own mother not to leave me with the guilt of allowing her to go on a walk and ending up dead somewhere.

Now, looking back on all of my mother's attempts to kill herself… it is so much clearer for me to assess them as attention seeking. She left the house right when she knew I would hear the door. Which she slammed instead of trying to quietly sneak away. She was always found under a tree somewhere close to home. Never having taken enough pills to complete the job. And she never took off when the opportunity would give her hours of time with no-one noticing.

She showed no emotion. Not even the sight and sounds of her only daughter falling to pieces as she cried out for her mommy, derailed her from her mission.

I managed to get close enough to her to grab her purse from her and make my way back inside. Only then did she come back in the doorway after me. And when I found the bottle of pills, the can of sprite and kitchen knife inside… she said nothing. Just glared at me. With a slight smirk on her face as she watched my heart sink to the floor.

It wasn't her anymore. It hadn't been her for a very long time. And if I dig really deep, I don't know if I've ever known who my mother is.

There were many times throughout my young life when my mom tried to leave us. But not one single time did she ever leave a note. No piece of paper to tell us she loves us. No apology for feeling that killing herself was her only option. Not a single sentence of explanation or attempt to release us of the guilt from it being any of our faults.

Nothing.

Through the muddled memories of my growing up; that fact remains painfully clear. It shaped the way I valued myself. It molded the image I saw when I looked in the mirror. I wasn't even worth the effort for her to leave a few words behind for.

After that day, I no longer went to visit her during her hospital stays. I stopped trying to paint a pretty picture out of her darkness. I decided I was not going to cuddle her during her moments of paranoia and hallucinations. And I would not give her anything of myself that she needed.

I killed myself in her story.

To this very day, she says her memory is bad and can't recall much if any of those times. I may never hear an apology from her. I may never get a single solid conversation out of her explaining what she was going through or feeling in those days.

But what I can come up with on my own, is that my poor mother has always felt empty. She has hated herself, starved herself to the point of hospitalizations and feeding tubes. Even ripping those tubes from her own belly. Her will to control her environment has caused her to be angry, obsessive, constantly sick for attention. She has always been too consumed by her demons to step outside and care for me.

Today, I feel sad for her. I wish she could have found her voice and told her own tale of pain and suffering. Oh how I longed for that connection with her throughout my own years of struggle. For her to say, "I understand." "I have felt that way too." I have yearned for any closeness with her. Any kind of bond. As a young child I scrambled to chase her light. Like a dog trailing at her owners ankles. As a teen I revolted against her. Hiding from any space she was in. knowing it would only leave me feeling unloved, unlovable and afraid. Afraid of finding myself in her eyes.

I have her eyes.

I am a woman born of a woman who knows nothing about healthy love. Love for herself. Love for another. It is not her fault. It is not my fault. It just is. I could sit in the shade of the cards that have been dealt and watch myself turn into the exact malnourished woman that I am speaking of. Or I can find a way to forgive without an apology. To relate without being related to. To love her without her being capable of returning that love in the same way.

I can heal.

In my healing I have gone through many different phases. Each one just as crucial as the next. I have found the things about her that I absolutely love. Her passion for the holidays and holiday traditions. I carry on those same traditions with my own children. I have wept at her feet in gratitude for those memories that she gave me as a girl. I am able to say thank you and mean it in every fiber of my being; for the parts of her that I treasure.

I can look at her pictures and separate her sickness from her beauty. Her amazing talent for music and melodies. Her gift at writing and singing those songs without fear. I miss her. It's funny how we can feel a loss from someone who has never really been present. Ultimately I am a motherless daughter.

But today, it is me who has made that choice for myself.

She didn't leave me. I left her.

I own it. I stand by it. I am proud of what that decision has done for my life. I don't set boundaries against anyone. I set them for me. For my children. For the space in which we thrive and run free from suffocation. Emotional abuse… because that is the true definition… abuse…. Will suck the air right from your lungs. It will steal the wind from beneath your wings. Boundaries must be set in order to continue healing.

Setting boundaries is the most freeing thing I have ever done for myself. I set boundaries with love; love for myself. Love for my children. Love for the life I have worked so hard to create.

Boundaries can have many definitions. But ultimately if they are repeatedly disrespected... you are left with two choices. To continue to exist in a life with toxic poison flowing into your spirit. Or you can completely detach. Detachment is not without its heartbreak. But it has been nothing like the continual hurt I have felt by keeping my parents in my life.

Co-dependency is defined as excessive emotional or psychological reliance on a partner or family member who requires support due to an illness or addiction. My dad will always choose to protect her sickness over anyone else. He will never see his own responsibilities for the absolute destitution in which they live. My parents have never chosen me over their own patterns of illnesses and addictions.

Never.

It would be a total lie if I told you that that simple fact doesn't crush me every single time I allow myself to be aware of it. It makes me angry and resentful. I feel heartbroken that they cannot see me as a precious child of their own love.

Love is something that can only be met as far as the other person has learned to meet themselves.

For them... that leaves very little to give.

And for me, that leaves a lot for me to acquire for myself. It is not an easy road, it has brought me terrifyingly close to death. I have had to figure out my own way to dig myself out of the shit I have learned. To unlearn everything I have been shown to believe. To believe about life. About myself.

To stop being apologetic for the space in which I exist! To know that I am worthy and have a lot to offer. Just because someone else isn't able or capable or willing to see it... does not mean that it doesn't exist! The things that I was shown as a little girl are unfortunate. They have devastated the natural flow in which a girl becomes a woman.

I feel it.

I scream at it. I cry and break open to let it all flow from my broken little-girl heart.

And most importantly… I unload the burdens that were never mine to carry and I left them on the front porch of my white picket-fenced childhood home. Which has freed up my arms to hold that little blonde-haired girl… To pick her up off the floor and twirl her around in the sunshine. And love her the way she was never loved before. To accept her and tell her she is not bad. None of that is her fault. She is love. She is beauty. She is strong and capable.

And I gave her permission to say all of the things she was never, ever… supposed to talk about.

"There is no greater agony than bearing an untold story inside of you."

-Maya Angelou

The Things We Don't Talk About

The experiences I had as a child eventually dampened out the spark that little girls possess. I wasn't daydreaming of princesses and unicorns; there were no crowns on my head or magic wands in my hands when I looked in the mirror. I spent a lot of time worrying.

Wondering.

Wondering why I couldn't fix what was broken in her? Why doesn't dad protect us? What did I do to make her cry so much? How can I make her proud of me? When will she be okay? Who can I talk to and what am I even allowed to say?

When you're young you don't realize the magnitude of your silence. The weight it bears on your self-worth. I felt angry. But anger was not allowed. I wanted to scream and cry. Instead I was taught to always smile. I watched other families and it was clear that mine was different. Maybe not from the outside… although I remember hearing other moms talk about why my mom was never available to pick me up from slumber parties. Or why I was never involved in any activities outside of school. They would whisper about their daughters never being invited over to my home.

But I could hear them. The white picket fence never truly fooled anyone but us, I guess.

But on the inside, everything was broken. We were all shattered in different ways. And no one ever talked about it. In my family, if you speak about something; bringing your feelings out into the open… the entire world will fall apart. She will fall apart. So we tip-toed quietly inside the walls of our house. And played our given roles on the outside. We had a golden rule:

There are things you just do not talk about.

Ever.

I became pregnant at 16. I was so scared. I told my boyfriend who said we would get married and everything would be ok. I tried to rest in his words. But I didn't want to be a mother, I was sure I was going to be a terrible one. Being raised in the religious strictness I was, abortion was murder. No exceptions. I couldn't do that. Could I? So I focused on this new life ahead. And a week later my boyfriend left me.

I was so alone. No one to talk to. No one would understand.

The Things We Don't Talk About

My mom was in a mental hospital at the time for attempting suicide again. It was a long stay, the longest I think she had ever been committed. I had stopped visiting her in hospitals a few years before that. A thought came to me that maybe this baby would give my mom something to want to live for. A purpose for her life. I needed a mom more than ever. Even a broken one. So I made the drive to visit her in the hospital. To tell her in person that I was pregnant and I needed her to live!

I was a girl who mothered her own mom. I was always the kid who was trying to ease her mom's suffering. I was always attempting to say or do something, anything… that would make her want to stay. I signed in to the nurses' station outside of the unit. It was a locked-down wing of the hospital. My mom had escaped the last hospital she was in. The security finding her on the side of the freeway. So they took no chances with her from then on.

I went through and sat down on a bench waiting for her to get out of a group she was in. My palms were sweating. To tell her I was pregnant meant also admitting I was having premarital sex. Which was a major sin in my home. But I was driven to tell the truth, driven by the hope that this was the biggest thing she had ever been presented with. A gift to change her focus on not wanting to live. She finally came out and sat down by me. If I could find the words to describe the level of detachment to her own daughter that she was conveying… I would write them. But it is indescribable. And the gaze in her eyes broke my terrified heart in half.

But this was it. I was going to go through with this pregnancy to save her from this nightmare she was living. So I told her. "Mom, I'm going to have a baby. I am all alone. And I need you. Your grandchild needs you. Please get better and come home." Now in hindsight and as a grown woman it was foolish for me to think that I was capable of healing my mom. But as a young teenage girl, I was hopeful. Aren't we all? She didn't say much. But she rarely does. We decided to wait and tell my dad when she came home.

A week or so later she was released to come home. We sat my dad down and told him. It went as well as it could have, she and I talked about babies and childbirth. Motherhood and her experiences with delivering my brother and I.

I even went out and bought a couple onesies. It was a connection to my mom and that was worth everything to me. It was a pretty amazing week of her and I sharing talks, spending time ... mother and daughter. A week is all she lasted. I drove up to my house to see cop cars. My dad standing in the driveway with the look I had seen many times before.

She was gone.

I ran upstairs and fell apart. I already knew that I wasn't enough for her. But now this baby wasn't either. I was shattered and scared to death. What was I doing? What was I thinking? I have no one. I have nothing. I called the clinic that moment and scheduled to terminate my pregnancy. My dad signed the paper. No one talked to me about it. Everyone was in disarray over my mother. I felt invisible. Unimportant. I thought I saw promise in her eyes. I thought I saw love.

I terminated that pregnancy. And I never talked about it. My dad never asked me how I was. My mom eventually came home from the hospital and she never mentioned the baby, my feelings, or even the horrible sin I had just committed. Nothing. I know pain. I know shame. And I know what it feels to just be a bird and fly away from myself. Leaving my physical body to fend for itself when things are just too terrible for me to absorb. That's what I did as a little girl. It is how I coped with my mom's erratic and confusing behavior. And it's how I managed to get through the process of the abortion.

I flew... but the memories and the guilt stayed. The words I never spoke, swirled around in my head like bullets.

And those are the things I carried in my heart. All throughout my life. Slowly allowing them to destroy me until all that I was left with was an empty shell of a woman. My life, if you can even call it that, became an existence soaked in shame. I made destructive decisions and chased anything that might numb my anguish.

I don't recall ever wanting to die. But I don't remember caring if I continued living either.

The shit that you're not allowed to talk about turns into the pain you won't allow yourself to talk about. It all eventually grows and transforms into your own secrets. Somehow you have now taken ownership and responsibility yet again for all the trauma you are protecting. And as you run from those demons, a mountain of wreckage swells and builds right behind you.

Everywhere you go.

It's kinda like in the movie Forest Gump. When he goes for his run across the country. He just keeps running and running... not really aware of all the people that begin to gather behind him as he makes his way through each state. And then one day, he stops and turns around... face to face with hundreds of people that were now following behind him. Then he says, "I'm tired, I think I'll go home now," and he has to begin walking towards the crowd in order to end his run.

When you finally drop all of the excuses, let go of all the tools you have been using in an attempt to protect the story you have been suffocating all along your roads in life... you will come face to face with the demons of your past. Who have never left you. They have been behind you all along.

Destroying everything you touch. Ruining your relationships with others. Disturbing any chance at peace with yourself. The secrets we keep must be told. The story of our suffering must be shared. There is no beauty in silence for the sake of appearing whole.

I became a perfect breeding ground for perfectionism.

Nothing about perfectionism leads you to feel anything close to perfect. In fact it leaves you feeling inadequate and constantly failing. I developed a very unhealthy relationship with food when I was around nine. Maybe it started much younger. My mother was always starving herself… I could never be as disciplined as she was.

Disciplined.

That is how I viewed it, I admired her ability to eat almost nothing. To waste away right before our eyes. I felt bigger than her. Bulky in comparison to her waif-like figure. I carried that into my school girl days. My feet were too big to share the shoes of my classmates. I was a lot taller than most of the girls around me. Bigger. Clumsier. I hated my face, my feet, my height. I remember bringing portioned controlled lunches in the fourth grade.

Portion control turned into skipping meals; which progressed into chewing food and then spitting it out before I swallowed. And when I was so hungry I couldn't help myself from swallowing, I would throw it up if I felt I had already eaten enough that day.

Eating became a signal to myself that I was a failure. Not eating made me feel a little bit in control.

But I seriously struggled with starvation. I was unsuccessful way more times than victorious. When you hate yourself so much you grab your skin and just cry out with disgust… there is a very serious problem brewing.

I never talked about it to anyone. And it came and went. Substances would ease my self-loathing for a while.

But I was always restless. Discontent with the skin I was in.

Today I have a daughter. She is just a baby, but I want her to blossom into whoever she is with confidence. There is enough pressure from the outside world for girls to look a certain way, express only specific emotions... behave in a way that society expects us to. It is my mission to create a home base; a solid foundation where she can always regain her footing in case she becomes lost in expectations.

There is no shaming of bodies in my house. You do not have to verbalize that you hate your body, for your children to pick up on the fact that you hate your body! You don't need to say out loud that you hate yourself, or your life, or your spouse... kids pick up on all of it anyways. And I don't want my children to suffer the way I did. No covering up of feelings. We talk about everything with my son and will do the same with my daughter. My daughter will have enough pressure as a woman without me adding to the weight she will carry with my own baggage.

I treat my body as if she is my daughter. I talk to myself as if I'm speaking to my daughter. Because in the end, it is exactly how my little girl will end up treating herself. The cycle stops here. Her story will be free to roam in my presence. No matter what it is.

I hid my emotions. I hid my insecurities. I covered up my shame. I began to create a picture of who I wanted everyone else to believe I was. After a while, the lies become who you are. The truth gets pushed so far back, it's almost impossible to conjure up.

I lost myself. I lost my voice. I always felt so apologetic for the space I took up. So unwanted, unneeded, unnecessary. I didn't fit in. I couldn't belong anywhere. Denying my own feelings. Suppressing my truth. The pain overtook me.

I cannot go back in time and stand up for myself. I cannot speak when I remained silent or run away when I chose to just be still. Nothing I do today can ever change what happened to me as a girl. But what I can do is change the way it has shaped me. I can feel what I should've been allowed to feel. I can tell my story... uninhibited by fear. I will walk through the forest of forgiveness.

Nothing that I speak of can ever hurt me again!

If you are broken... break! If you are angry... scream. If you feel overwhelming grief... my God, cry! You will not go over the edge of sanity by allowing yourself to open up. The ocean of sadness will not drown you. But silence will.

I can now say that what I experienced as a blonde pig-tailed little girl... was not my fault! I know that in every cell of my body. I deserved to be loved and protected, cherished and nurtured. I needed to be shown what a woman with love for herself and love in her heart for me.. looked like. It's not blaming or shaming anyone from my past. In fact, I feel a sense of sorrow for them.

And I take back what they took. I give myself back the freedom to be a woman. To be as powerful and fluid as water. To weep when I feel overcome with sadness. To march when I feel empowered to make a stand. I dance when I hear the music of my soul.

I will allow myself to sit with the feelings of that little girl when they come. I can pick her up and hold her through them. We will be ok. She is safe with me. And I am safe to swim in whatever waters she needs to in order to heal.

The things we carry with us from childhood become more than just memories in our minds. The sounds and smells; sensations and images all come over me at once. They take me over completely. It is more than a thought of a time long past.

It is a feeling all throughout my being. A slightly nauseating flow of emotions that can leave me out of breath. They are less frequent now and don't last as long as they once did. It may be something I always have with me. But it does not need to define me. Carrying such deep untold secrets for so many years slowly turned them into parts of my body. An unsteadiness in my footing. A disfigured reflection in the mirror. And as I walked through my life into adulthood, my steps took me down some very dark roads.

I don't think there is a cut-and-dry age of when a child is no longer a child. When one is now responsible for their choices. It can be difficult for me, even today… to find a clear moment when I crossed the bridge into womanhood. But I would say it was around sixteen or seventeen when I became aware of ways I could be better… do better; cope better.

But I did not choose them. It's pretty monumental when I think about it. There I was, filled with the grief of a child, making my way into what should have been the grace of a woman. It is then that I now take complete ownership of my decisions.

It was then that I met the beast.

*"Numbing the pain
For a while
Will make it worse
when you finally
feel it."*

-J.K. Rowling

The Animal

"How did I get here?"

I can't even count how many times I asked myself that question. Sitting in courtrooms, shackles on my wrists and ankles waiting for a judge to hear my cases. The smell of heroin seeping from pores as I drip with sweat in withdrawal. Wanting to claw out of my dirty body. Everything ached. Just the feeling of clothes on my body made my skin hurt so bad. And the anxiety… my stomach was sick, my heart pumped so fast.

Just sitting there time and time again. Feeling like an absolute piece of shit as I watched the public defenders in front of me chatting about their weekends or their upcoming plans. Giggling and full of life. I could smell their perfume as they walked past me. I would look at their shoes and their eye shadow and just want to scream out, "Hey! I used to be just like you. I am a person too!" Being arrested and processed into jail is such a degrading experience. The first few times I was taken into custody, I could always count on at least a handful of officers having heart to hearts with me.

"How did you get here?" Telling me I didn't belong in jail, that I was too pretty, had too much potential.

They stopped saying that over the years I spent in my addiction. I guess I began looking like a junkie should look. Behaving like an addict whose life is out of control is supposed to act. They would welcome me back as they made a joke about fucking up again. And put me in a solitary holding cell as an act of kindness since the "heroin junkie" was back and would be dope sick soon.

In my town, the county jail doesn't house women. So in the middle of the night, any females who weren't released or bailed out would get shackled together and bussed to different neighboring county jails to be housed until their court dates began. During those two-hour bus rides to and from court, I would stare out the window and down into the cars on the roads. Watching people drive with their coffees and their nice clothes. Passing up places and landmarks that I had memories of back when I was once a regular person.

Before I was who I became.

I don't think anyone dreams of becoming a drug addict when they grow up. It certainly wasn't my life goal. I can remember wanting to be a veterinarian. I loved animals. Animals are so healing, their love is unconditional and you can count on them to never stop being happy to see you. I was smart enough in school to have made that dream an absolute reality. But what happened turned out to be quite different than I could've ever imagined.

When I was around twelve, a friend of mine had a ranch with a guest house we would hang out in. one day we went exploring and found vodka in a cupboard. Curious as most pre-teens are, we poured ourselves some glasses and drank. I can remember so vividly the warmth of the alcohol in my stomach. And then a calmness, a steadiness in my chaotic insides that began moving over my body a few minutes later.

Peace.

I had never known serenity before that day. She got giggly and started acting funny. I got quiet. My brokenness felt whole. My feet no longer felt too big. My body didn't look bulky and awkward. The bullying voices of insecurities and memories of my shame stopped cold. I was fucking free! It was like a miracle! To step outside of my tortured mind, even for a few hours was like nothing else I had ever experienced. I'm sure for her it was just a fun afternoon. But for me, it was like the first taste of blood for a vampire.

I wanted more.

We passed out on the couches and woke to her mom calling us to take me home. Home? I didn't want to go home! Home was a disoriented mess of emotions that I felt so incapable of surviving. I was a little sick to my stomach from the vodka… and I wanted to do it again! I wanted to feel free forever. I never wanted to leave that guest house with that bottle of liquid liberty.

My home life was chaotic. My hormones and feelings for boys created a lot of weird thoughts about the kind of girl I was when I was younger. I think becoming a teenage girl in a high school full of horny boys brought some repressed memories to the forefront. I felt overcome with emotions.

I found acceptance in alcohol and marijuana. I felt like I finally belonged anywhere I went. Most kids party on the weekends. I have never used or drank to party. I used to survive. I wanted relief. Relief from myself. I was seeking to erase the memories of all the times I used my little girl body as a way to feel special. I drank away my mother's madness, I snorted up my insecurities, I smoked my tortured insides up until they were numb. And I wanted it all the time. So I quickly found myself around the kids who did more hardcore drugs. Meth, acid, mushrooms. And I consumed it all.

I believe for a moment in time, drugs and alcohol may have saved my life. The depression and anxiety; shame and body image issues were becoming increasingly unbearable. I wanted to claw out of my skin. To stop breathing out of my own mouth. I wanted to run so far that the memories would not be able to find me. It is possible, that I may have followed in my mom's footsteps and attempted to end it all.

I ran away from home at fifteen. Quit school. Lived in a flop house of older men and teenage runaways and did so much meth I became psychotic. Paranoid. I was afraid a lot. Unsure of what was going on around me. Starving. Only water with lemon to drink a lot of the time. Man was I sick.

My memories of this time in my life are hazy at best. I don't trust my recollection of what happened. But I know I was confused and my perception of the world around me was distorted and scary. Seeing people that I'm not sure were really there. Hearing noises that no one else seemed to hear.

And the men. Dangerous and disgusting. But something in me sought out the worst of the worst. I set out on a mission to prove to the world that no one would ever intimidate me again. I hid any fear I had. I put myself in terrible situations on purpose just to prove to myself that I could handle it. I was in charge. Even if I was out of control.

I think when you grow up feeling so out of control over everything… you crave some kind of order. Even if it's chaotic order. At least it's your own. It was mine. No one was going to touch me unless I wanted them to. No one was going to leave me before I left them. I would self-destruct before I ever allowed anyone else to destroy me.

I was arrested. My parents came to pick me up. I was a fucking mess.

Somehow I managed to get my life together and graduate from home studies. I went to cosmetology school and began creating a normal life for myself. Alcohol never left me. I drank wine like all classy and successful women are supposed to. I fell into the slippery trap of an image of what a woman is supposed to look like.

I hated myself. I drank.

I fell in love with all the wrong guys. I drank. I got credit cards and new cars. I drank. I shopped. I drank. I tried to lose weight. I drank. I drank and drank and drank. And it grew and grew until I drank over everything and all the time. I never talked about it, I never thought about it. I just didn't want to be me.

Somewhere at some point I crossed that invisible bridge. The bridge that lies between a normal drinker and an alcoholic. And the truth is, you really don't have an inclination that you are approaching it until you are too far. You don't come to understand you are in real trouble until you are. On the outside I was slowly deteriorating. On the inside, alcohol wasn't enough anymore. It wasn't taking away the pain.

In a twist of fate, bad luck... bad timing maybe; I had a wisdom tooth removed. I was given Vicodin.

And again the beast in my soul was satisfied. Opiates took my life like a thief in the night. That control I craved was gone. I was sick with them. Sick without them. I would soon lose my job. Lose my apartment. Lose my friends. Throw away my dignity and self-respect. I was so alone.

I had the rest of my wisdom teeth pulled for no reason. Procedures on my knees that I didn't need. I had to buy them from people who sold their prescriptions. I ran out of doctors to shop from. I ran out of money to buy the pills on the street. I lied to get whatever I could find. I sold them to get what I could take out of the profit. I found myself homeless.

The period of time between trying to keep my life together and just completely surrendering to my addiction and giving it all up... was absolute hell. Having one foot in my old life and the rest of me slowly being consumed by the drug life, was a battle I couldn't keep up for long. Being sick and searching for whatever opiates I could find.

Making excuses after excuses to friends for any pills they may have had left over from surgeries.

One day I remember being in such terrible withdrawals and laying on the couch of this meth dealer I was staying with. He had a friend show up to bring me something. But what he brought was not pills. It was heroin. I was fucking desperate for relief. I let him inject my vein in my arm. The needle didn't even hurt. And instantly I was numb.

I only had to watch him give me that one shot. I was on my own and on my way into the deepest darkest world of drugs and crime from that moment on. I reunited with my old friend meth. Mixing the two evils on a spoon day after day after day. I was a slave. A slave to the beast. My beast speaks to me in a beautiful voice. She is reassuring and convincing that everything is fine. She blinds me to the absolute horror of my reality. She kisses all my wounds better. She is exquisite and sneaky. I was powerless against her.

I gave her everything that ever mattered to me without even realizing it was gone. I was willing to do anything she asked of me as long as she kept me well. Because that's what happens after a while of being a heroin addict. You use to get well. To feel human. The withdrawals are excruciating and last for days to weeks. Then the psychological and emotional sickness really kicks in. It is a long and horrific process.

How does a girl go from doing hair in a nice salon and sipping wine with her beautiful friends… to living in flop houses full of criminals; robbing homes, stealing from stores, smuggling weapons across the border? Desperate and destitute. On the run from the law, arrested over and over again.

It happens.

It happened to me.

I put myself in such incredibly dangerous situations with ridiculously dangerous guys. Trying to gain a feeling of empowerment. A feeling I had never known. To feel empowered as a woman. To walk with confidence and feel respected by the people around me. To feel valued. The truth though, was that I was hustling for my worthiness. Just as I did as a girl. Fighting for love in any way I could. On my hands and knees, searching for any scraps of love and respect people would throw at my bloody feet.

I was almost killed trying to prove my value to a very violent guy I dated. I would wake up in motel rooms with bullets all around my body on the bed. He was trying to put fear into me. I didn't heed the warnings. I pushed him and confronted every single act of aggression. Fear made me confront him harder, push him further. I eventually managed to push him into the arms of another girl. I am very good at that. Crossing the line of acting tough and becoming too aggressive. Pushing people away on the outside as I'm begging for them to stay on the inside.

And then I pushed him even further by falling in love with his friend.

He was kind; too sweet to be living the lifestyle we were living. He made me feel loved. A little bit safe to be like a girl again. We talked about leaving the lifestyle, the goals we had and the dreams of a family and a home without all of this madness. He loved me. I started to dream again. And that love gave me a glimmer of hope for my life. That maybe I still had a chance to be happy. I didn't want to live my life without him.

But my ex didn't like that.

One day he came over and called me down to talk to him. I went. I was not going to show fear to anyone. But I was terrified. He grabbed me and tried to kidnap me. I swear to you that God was looking out for me. Because for some reason his friend wouldn't drive despite his yelling at him to take off with me; hanging half way out of this van. A girl saw the commotion and grabbed my arm trying to help me. After a few seconds in a tug of war with my life, he eventually let go and they sped off.

He returned that night. Sneaking into the apartment and waiting in the dark. When I came out into the hallway he grabbed me from behind and had a knife to my throat. I will never forget the sound of his voice in my ear. Pleading for me to just leave with him so we could talk. There have been more times than I can even wrap my head around… when God has come to my rescue. A guy came out after hearing the scuffling in the hall. My ex punched me in the face so hard I flew down the hall and against the bathroom wall.

One day later, he asked my sweet boyfriend for a ride. My ex told him to drive to a secluded area and he stabbed the first guy who had been kind to me in a very long time; thirty-two times, with the very same knife he had held to my throat the night before; and left him to die all alone in the hills.

When I think about how easily that could've been me… would have been my body lying in the cold night dying had he succeeded in taking me… had I not been rescued by two people who really showed up out of nowhere… I get really emotional. I was the girl who never backed down no matter what fears I felt inside. I was the girl on a death mission to prove myself.

A year later, he went to trial. I was called to testify. I was in custody at the time so I had no choice but to take the stand. When I was asked questions about everything I knew about the crime… I did what I have always done best.

I said nothing.

I looked my old boyfriend in the eyes as he sat in the defense chair… and I denied everything that was presented to me. I lied. I disowned my truth. I betrayed my sweet boyfriend and I betrayed myself.

I am a secret keeper. I have been groomed to swallow my own self-worth and protect the ugliest of truths.

Thankfully the prosecution was not relying on my testimony and the lunatic was sentenced 25 years to life. He was only twenty-six. I think about him sometimes. How he too lost his life that day. Drugs and mental illness robbed him of all his possibilities. Addiction will create demons out of angels. Criminals out of kind people. And in this case, a killer out of a friend.

I think back to how I pushed and pushed him despite seeing he was losing his mind.

I have spent many sleepless nights crying in the pillow to my love in heaven. Asking for his forgiveness. I believe he understands that I was not the woman I am today. I was broken. Unable to speak. Unsure of my power.

I was afraid.

And that is the truth of all of my tough-girl behavior. All of my pushing the envelope… pushing people away before they could leave me. Because not even my own mommy wanted to be with me. So I knew no one else could truly love me. I was tainted. Ugly. Disfigured by molestation and shame.

I didn't love me. How could I?

Addiction does not discriminate. It does not care if you have a career or children. It doesn't only affect those who are underprivileged or unloved. Addiction will creep up to you in a classy bar. It will appear as a savior in shiny armor. It will promise you peace and security. She swore to me that she was the answer to all of my suffering, all of my anger and resentments. She promised to wash me clean and leave me never needing to be held.

I believed her.

I was her slave for many years. Investing my life in all that she offered. I didn't know who I was without her. I lost who I was with her. And eventually my addiction and I pushed the envelopes of the system so hard that they sent us to prison.

Nothing could have prepared me for what lies behind a prisons walls. The women serving time since I was a child. The ones who will never see their freedom returned to them. Wounded people just bleeding all over everyone around them. Prison is like an alternate dimension.

With laws and behaviors that would make no sense to the outside world. But in there, it is a way of survival. The routines day after day after day. The dramas of high school age proportions yet with sometimes fatal consequences.

I could tell so many stories of the women and experiences I had in there, but there is one moment above all the rest that I will never forget, and more importantly I will never regret.

I was sitting in my cell after a walk in the yard. I looked around at the concrete walls that enclosed me. My metal bunk and my metal locker. I had nothing. The emptiness of my life. The hopelessness of my future. The sounds of women yelling at each other in their cells, the smells of the prison floors... everything started spinning and swirling.

And then all of the sound left the room.

Call it a spiritual experience. Call it God. Call it an epiphany. But I heard a voice in my heart. Have you ever heard with your heart? It's sound mixed with sensation. It was a voice. Not mine. And not my addiction. And that voice said four words;

"*This*... is your life."

This is my life. This was gonna be my life forever if I don't take myself back! No one was waiting for me. Time had not stopped without me. People were living. Getting married. Having kids and careers. Wearing perfume and bracelets and bathing suits in the sun.

This is *my* life.

I was thirty-four years old. With nothing to show for it but a long felony record, track marks on my neck, a locker full of shit that didn't matter and a head full of regrets. In that moment, I chose life. I chose me. I chose to face and walk through whatever fire was awaiting me. I made the decision on that day to reclaim myself from the beast. From my past. From the ungodly man. From the lunatic. To put down what I was carrying for my mom and find the strength to pick up the pieces of my soul that were scattered on the floor.

The Animal

I dreamed of becoming a veterinarian as a little girl. But what I had become was an animal.

Existing in the most barbaric of circumstances. Eating from garbage cans. Filthy and dirty. Urinating on the streets. Stealing from everywhere and everyone I came in contact with. Accepting the scraps of humanity that were tossed my way. Running.

Addiction knows no bounds. It takes and takes until you are dead. It will not stop. You will give everything of yourself away to avoid the having to be aware of what has happened to your life, to your self-respect.

I believe God saved my life that day sitting on my prison bunk.

Call it whatever you are comfortable with. I call it divine intervention. He intervened on my piece of shit life and gave me the courage to make the most frightening decision I had ever made before. I chose to stop running. To turn around and make a sound. I would like to say that I roared at my demons like a mighty lion. But in truth my voice was a barely audible squeal.

Broken and sick. Pummeled by and defeated by addiction. Locked away in prison. Cut off from the real world. But it was something, a start. A small victory over my life. I was shaken but standing.

Recovery has given me a life that is worth living. A life that has become worth saving. I am worthy of recovery. Everyone is worthy of taking back their lives from the depths of hell that addiction brings you to. Recovery has delivered all the promises that my beast presented to me.

Even when I had nothing to give, nothing to say, nowhere to turn… recovery and the people in it have always invited me in. They have loved me until I was able to love myself. Abstaining from drugs and alcohol was the first step to putting the pieces of myself back together. Being sober has given me clarity to see my past for what it was, my present for what it is, and my future for what it can be.

The Animal

I have a storm under my skin. It is a grace filled ocean with hope and truth raging in its seas. As I heal, it grows. It calls to me. I feel the pull of the wind and the breeze blows through me like freedom.

This is my life. I am free. Free to speak. Free to feel. Free to explore. Free to carry on.

And today, I am awake.

"In order for forgiveness to happen, something must die."

-Brene Brown

The Things We Lay To Rest

There will be many paths you take along the road to healing. The truth is, being a survivor of abuse, addictions and oppressions is a personal journey that spans over a lifetime. It all brings us to the same place. A place that is filled with just ourselves; where there is stillness. A place where we are surrounded by the truths we do not want to hear, the faces we do not want to see, the voices that have been screaming at us that we can no longer tune out.

There will be a lot of letting go. Letting go of the things that masked our shame. Letting go of who we thought we were. Letting go of the past to make a way for a future.

Letting go is not releasing responsibility. Its accepting what already is. Letting go is not condoning. The experiences do not need your permission, they have already happened. No amount of struggle or thinking or plotting can ever turn back time! You can wrestle with it until you die. You may even miss your entire life by existing in a time that has long since been over.

In order to let go... we must lay to rest those parts that are no longer serving us.

I had to let go of always trying to be in control of how the world viewed me. In being so committed to pretending I was someone I was not, I lost sight of how I saw myself. I lost connection to my own soul. I had to get out of my survival mode and let people see the real me. I was not on the streets anymore or in prison... I had grown into a woman who need not be afraid of the things that happened to me as a little girl. I let go of the glorification of toughness and the invincibility I hid behind. Vulnerability is fucking terrifying! But hanging on to the façade of me was a death sentence. Hanging on to all of the mistakes I had made, the sins I had committed, and the things I had endured was only keeping me sick.

I had to forgive.

I had built a cage of anger and hardness all around me. I hated women. I hated being a woman. I didn't want to be soft, vulnerable, emotional. I was a gaping wound walking around in a body I despised. I didn't want to heal. I honestly didn't even know what that looked like. I believed that women cried as a way to manipulate men. I wanted to stay in my cage of pain and not let anyone know who I was. Because if they knew... surely they would no longer respect me. I was sure they would try to victimize me in some way.

I did not just open up like a flower in the morning sunshine when I got clean and sober. Quite the opposite actually. Taking away the drugs and alcohol left me bleeding and open and laying naked in a riverbed of shame, guilt, fear... anger. So much anger. It took me years to understand that it was sorrow. I was sad, I was hurt. I felt fucking cheated out of my childhood. I was seeing how many years I had tossed away in an effort to run from grief.

I'd had enough. It had to die.

They say there are five stages to death; for the person who is dying and for those who have to grieve a loved one who is passing or has passed:

Denial. Anger. Bargaining. Depression. Acceptance.

It is more than ironic that these are the exact phases you will walk through in the process of forgiveness.

Denial has to be the most destructive way to cope with life's truths. Running from the realities of your life will cost you more than anything else. The things I had to do in order to remain in denial almost cost me my life so many times. There was not enough sand to bury the memories of my childhood, not enough water to drown out the voices of shame and my own insignificance in this world. There are not enough drugs to numb the pain of all of years I abused myself.

All of the years I spent on my hands and knees scrounging around for little scraps of love that I was able to find. Blaming myself. Labeling myself as dirty and unlovable.

Pain. Pain is so fucking necessary in order to heal. There are a million ways to try and avoid it. But there is only one way to truly be free of it… and that is to sit with it and feel it. All of it. The first pain I had to hold was the pain of my childhood. It hurts to face the facts. To stop blaming myself for the way I was loved. To look at my memories and come to terms with the truth that I was abused. By people who were supposed to love me, protect me, people who were meant to show me that life was good and beautiful and I was strong enough to do whatever I dreamt of.

I almost threw away my future so many times trying to avoid that truth. It was easier for me to hate myself and hold myself responsible than to say the words out loud… "I was not loved the way I should have been by my parents." "I was targeted and abused by a man who was supposed to teach me the ways of God." "I was not believed." "I was discarded." "I was no one's priority."

Just voicing those words caused me so much gut-wrenching sorrow.

But I sat with them, and sometimes I still have to lay down and say them. Hold those truths like a baby who needs to be consoled. To keep ownership of my story. To remain grounded in my truth. If I don't stay close to the voice I have finally found... I begin to retreat back into denial.

It is scary to face yourself... To face the truth of your childhood. And the painful reality of all of the years you have dismissed ownership of your own demise.

The truth will always find you!

You cannot fix what you are unwilling to face. You will continue to bleed all over yourself and everyone who you come in contact with.

No matter how far or fast you try to run... you will always return to yourself. No matter how much money you spend... peace in your heart cannot be bought. There is no drug or drink on this earth that is capable of permanently erasing your pain. You can spend all your time focusing on the broken parts of other people... but it will never make you whole.

When you finally get tired of your own shit, it all has to fall away.

Once you are willing to look at things as they really are, it can leave you really fucking angry! Angry at the ways you have been cheated of the childhood that was a God-given time of play and safety. Rage. Rage at the people involved in robbing you of those years.

Then there is the anger at yourself. For all of the years you carried it all with you and destroyed your life. Contaminated your body. Gave your heart to anyone who even showed the slightest interest. Begging for your self-worth, as if it could come from other people.

I think anger is something people try to push away too quickly. And I think that anger is something people try to stay with too long to avoid the real emotion lying just below. I was not allowed to express anger as a child. So I suppressed it, suffocated in it. Until I became a hostage to it. Here's the truth about anger, you have to consciously try to hang on to it. Because it will attempt to leave on its own in time. But what you are left with is grief.

Incredible grief.

And grief is consuming. Deep heartbreaking sadness can be the hardest feeling to sit with. Grief came over me like waves in the ocean. I couldn't catch my breath. The kind of grieving that physically hurt.

So I bargained.

Tried to alleviate it as fast as possible. Begged and pleaded with God to remove it from me so I wouldn't have to face it... Read positive quotes and meditated. Acted as if I was healed. But true skin-to-bone healing is not pretty. It's messy and chaotic. I could not afford to feed my numbness any longer. I had to feed my healing. I ate and slept with it. I cried and screamed. I wrote it out and rode it out. Sometimes I isolated with it and other times I shared it.

Healing takes time. A lot of time! There is no set timeline for how long a person should take to recover. I'm still healing. Maybe that's a journey I will always be on. But it's a much more manageable process today. In the beginning I was facing years and years of anger and grief, denial and destruction. I'm not gonna lie, it was a lot. And I would find myself sinking into deep depression.

It is difficult to see the light when you are walking through so many years of avoided darkness. Avoiding my darkness only fueled my suffering. And I was suffering! I wanted to give up. I wanted to stop feeling, stop crying, even stop living. But I had come so fucking far! I had so much sorrow inside and I thought it would kill me. Here's the funny thing about emotions... no matter how awful and treacherous the road is to walk through them... they will never kill you the way avoiding them will.

Knowing I never wanted to live the way I once lived; walking the streets, shooting up in bathrooms, dope sick and hopeless... completely soaked in shame to the point of living without basic humanity. Begging for love. Begging for respect. Hiding from mirrors because the sight of me was too much to bare. The alternative to walking through the forest of my feelings was to lie down and let the despair take me over.

If you want the past to define you, then go ahead and avoid forgiveness. I promise you, you will live trapped by your pain for the rest of your days. But that was something I could not accept.

So I accepted it all.

Acceptance is freeing. It's like waving the white flag at all of the destruction and standing on top of the rubble of your wasted dreams and surrendering to what was. I can never go back and undo all of the terrible ways I treated myself. I can't rewind time and never take that first drink or drug. There is no amount of mourning that will ever change all of the despicable crimes I committed. As much as I sat and replayed over and over again all the times I was too afraid to speak up; too beaten down to find my own way to stand. I can stare at my imperfections all day long... becoming overcome with disgust by my body won't change my body! And as much as I wish I could, I can't ride in a time machine back in time with some magic medicine to cure my mom.

But what I absolutely could do, is let it all be just as it already is. First just the experiences. Then as it felt like a natural progression... The people in those experiences. For me, this is the way forgiveness flows best. If I'm still hanging on to the experiences then it's impossible for me to release the people involved. Including myself. I could grab the pen of my life and rewrite the script of my future.

This is my life.

I forgive myself for choosing to be someone I was not; a hundred times over. I forgive myself for running when I should have stayed and fought. I forgive myself for shrinking when I could have grown, for hurting people because I was wounded, and I accept that I was a lost girl who never believed in the woman she could have been so long ago. I release myself from swallowing my words when they could have saved me. I apologized to my body for abusing her; to the woman inside of me for hating her.

I forgave my mother. She did the best that she could with what she was struggling with. Would I have existed in the same way she has? Probably not. But I am a different woman. And a huge part of that is because of my mom. She birthed a warrior. She may not have showed me a lot of love and stability, but she showed me how to fight for myself. I am a fiercely loving person today from being unloved. I learned how to find my own sunlit path by sitting so many years under her shadow.

I forgive the people from the church. I am working on thorough forgiveness of the man who hurt me.... but I completely forgive the experiences. And I am certain he is living with so many demons that he will never be able to rectify his peace. Only a very hurt person or a very sick person abuses other people. Especially children. And although he hurt me, my family and so many other families... there were men above him that were inflicting their own sickness onto him. I let go of all my experiences in Alabama. It is my story and my truth to do with whatever I feel is best for me. For now, I am at peace knowing I was a victim of a very disturbed group of people. I was an innocent child, seeking love from a pack of wolves.

Forgiveness is hard. It comes in waves. It comes in layers. You can't force it, yet it's imperative not to fight it. Letting the past die gives life to the future. Laying down all the excess baggage gives your arms room and strength to pick up the things that are yours to carry home.

Forgiveness does not have to mean re-entry. My family exists from the very same wounds and dysfunctional abusive behaviors they always have. I chose to set boundaries in order for me to thrive in my own life. I love them very much but from a very safe distance. My heart is always open if they ever choose to take responsibility for the way they navigate through life.

Generations of pain will continue until someone finally stands up, turns around and faces it all.

That person is me.

There was no magical moment that forgiveness gave me. There was no confetti thrown at my feet or parade in my honor.

There was no apology.

Forgiveness is for me. It is for my future and has nothing to do with the past. Nothing! The more compassion I feel for and show myself, the less compassion I crave from anyone else.

It was just me. Alone. Slowly burying the parts of my life that I no longer needed to hold on to!

And grabbing strength from each and every sorrow I ever endured. I am who I am because of it all. I am a soldier of the truth, the warrior in my story. The girl of my past has transformed into a woman of honor and respect. I know shame. I know resentments. I know abuse and I know abandonment. I know addiction and destitution. I also know redemption and recovery. I know the sound of my voice and the feel of the soil under my firmly planted feet. I know motherhood and what love truly is.

When I became pregnant with my son, I was terrified of the kind of mother I would be. I was overwhelmed with doubt in myself. What if I wasn't capable of loving a child the way he deserved? What if the things I went through as a child turned me into a pervert somehow and I ended up doing something unspeakable to him?

I came face to face with my fears of being a woman in this world as my belly grew. It was a real battle for me to allow myself to be free in that pregnancy. Nothing screams femininity like pregnancy. I hid myself away more often than not. I avoided having pictures taken. I didn't document those first movements or the ways in which my body slowly changed. It brought me so much shame. Not the pregnancy itself and not my son inside my womb, but the inability to present myself as a hard core fighter. I was forced to get into acceptance of my feminine being; and fast! I regret how much I missed of that pregnancy due to my struggle with letting my survival skills die. But it was part of my journey to what ended up so beautiful!

The minute they laid that sweet baby on my chest all my fears went away. I knew love. I understood in that moment that yes, I am my mother's daughter... but my child does not belong to my mother.

Four years later I became pregnant with a girl. I had come so far! I loved my beautiful belly. I soaked in my womanhood and all that it entails. I want my daughter to respect herself... so I found an even deeper level of self-love.

I apologized to my body for hating her. I forgave myself for disrespecting her.

I took all the dirt and sludge and spun it into gold. I have rebuilt resentments and anger into a truth that can help other people rise from their own silence. I took my self-hatred and grew a garden of self-respect. An example of fierce femininity. I speak for women who are oppressed by their own fears. Women who have been told for so long that it is all their fault, that they should just get over it and move on. Those who have grown weary of fighting to appear as someone other than themselves.

I no longer have time to talk about comparison or criticism. I don't care about flashy bullshit used to seek attention. I want authenticity and rawness. I want my children to be whole and free to exist from their hearts.

I swim in my womanhood. I laid to rest the tough shell I hid behind. My softness is much more resilient. I embrace her. I stand with her. I stand with all women in our beautiful openness for love and life. We are child-raising warriors. I want to walk this earth as a woman in all her glory. I bloom from the grave of the abused girl I have lovingly laid to rest. I wear all of the experiences that she went through, all of the battles I fought to silence her... as a beautiful crown on top of my head.

I will write and speak fire until it is every breath that I breathe. I am going to write about the hard stuff, the destruction and despair; the reckoning and resurrection.

I will live my truth whether I'm weeping or exuding joy. Whether I'm angry or serene. I will be courageous and heal out loud!

Because I'm not the odd one out… I am the one who got away.

No one can ever hide the story of me away…

ever again.

*"They asked her,
How did you free yourself?*

*She answered,
By embracing my own power."*

-Yung Pueblo

The Things We Hold On To

I have shivered under the chill of shame. My head in my hands, begging for relief from myself. I know isolation. I know suffering. I have walked away from my own body; leaving her to be ravaged by whatever and whoever may happen to trip over me. I have abandoned truth in search of more comfortable lies.

I know oppression. And my God do I know sorrow. And it is these very same things that I have known so well… this pain that I so wanted to be taken from, all of it…

They are the very things I now hold on to.

I am whole. Though you can still see the parts of me that were once damaged. They are the honest parts of my past that should not be hidden. It is in those cracks where you will find the treasures of who I am. There is nothing exquisite about how they got there, but the mere fact that I remain whole is what makes them art.

Releasing the past gives life to the future. I have laid those fragile broken girls to rest but I will forever hang on to their memories, they live on forever. Inside of me. Their brokenness gives flight to my wings. I fly high above their graves and honor them as I soar through this life. Redeemed!

I am more beautiful for having been broken. I bloom from the pain. I am making a beautiful home out of the parts of myself I once believed were unworthy of existing.

As you make the steps through your past, grabbing every single shattered piece of yourself that you have surrendered along the way… and take ownership back over it all; the power locked inside all of that pain can transform your entire life. It is not to be discarded! My story of brokenness and shame have been rewritten into a beautiful love letter to myself. A serenade to anyone who is gasping for air as they suffocate in their own silence!

Hope is the magic sauce of life!

I hold on.

I hold on to hope, I hold space for those who need a place to safely set their burdens down and pick the pieces of their lives. I hold on to the woman I have found and all the women I still have yet to meet.

Hold on to vulnerability. Embrace it all! I was born to love, to provide a foundation for my children. We were born to be loved. We learn the strengths of our flames from all of the moments it was almost extinguished… I have no intentions of shrinking my fire; no matter how hot it burns. Nothing defines me that I do not grant permission to.

These things aren't easy. But we are made to do hard things. The power of the human spirit to overcome is an incredible thing! We are made to do it with the grace that we feel inside of our beautiful bones. We stretch, we crack, we break… we weep and cry out… But we do not lay down and die.

I feel so grateful today to be alive to tell my story. There is really no earthly explanation for it. Grace. Grace meets us when we are the most broken. I believe in miracles. I see them and know them. I am one. I believe in redemption. Into spinning shit into pure gold. I trust in recovery and the hope that exists there! The promises are real and true. The obsession to use and drink has been lifted from me. I hold on to the memories of my destruction so I never fall into the trap of forgetting what happens to me when I choose to check out of my life. But I keep my eyes on the horizon ahead.

I am awake.

Turning my head away from anything that burns inside of me is to die. Silence is no longer an option. I gave myself permission to say all of the things that my heart needs to release. I release my truth and let freedom ring from my voice. My wounds no longer bleed. They are invincible scars that I will never ask to disappear.

I used to pray that God would take all of my memories from me. I would cry in the middle of the night for a new life… To start brand new. The times I spent homeless on the streets, sleeping in cars… sometimes in such severe withdrawals I would be on my knees throwing up in the dirt. Sweating and shaking. Begging to just be someone else! Anyone else but me. I have longed to be asleep to who I was. Shame.

There is no way to turn your back to shame. You can avoid guilt. You can shove grief down with anger. Drugs and alcohol, risky behavior can drown out loneliness and sorrow. But shame. Shame fills you with a relentless unwavering yearning to be someone else. But the truth is… everything that I have ever been through has built me to be the woman I am today! Even taking away one thing would change who I have become. And today, I don't want to be anyone other than me!

I am worthy.

Worthy of recovery and respect. I am worthy of life and love and leaning into all that I feel called to explore. I am worthy of true friendships and a sisterhood of women who know their own worth. I can trust myself and my judgements to detach from anyone that wants to throw shade on my sunlight. I honor my emotions, I validate my fears. I walk through whatever is ahead because I believe in myself; from bone to skin. We are worthy, we are enough, we are resilient and I believe we can move mountains!

I am worthy of love and setting boundaries to protect that love. I don't want to hurt my family. I have no intentions to hurt anyone. My heart breaks over the loss of them in my life. But I had no peace. My children are worthy of a healthy momma. They don't need to witness their mom being emotionally and psychologically tormented by anyone. I know what it's like to grow up in turmoil. I refuse to repeat that in my life today. It's not an easy pill to swallow, but you can't be medicine to people who are committed to remaining sick.

I know they don't understand, they don't see anything they do as anything more than a reaction to their own victimization at the hands of life. When people live a certain way for so many years, it becomes normal. Acceptable. I hold on to my new normal. I love my children and our future more than I'm concerned about them or anyone else understanding my journey. Being part of that madness had to come to an end.

I deserve to be loved and free to flourish. I deserve to speak about my pain however I see fit. I don't need to drop it or just forget about it. They ask me, "Why do you remember so much?" "Why can't you just move on?" They want me to be their medicine, to help them hide their secrets. But in the end, nothing ever helped them. All that it ever did was slowly kill me. So I detached.

Detaching from my family is not because I hate them. It is because I finally love me enough! I am not going to say that it doesn't hurt. It does, I think it hurts us all. But it is the only way I am able to heal my life. I was a house built from self-doubt and self-loathing. I cannot raise healthy children in a house like that. I cannot walk this earth consumed by their refusal to take any steps to get better. Some people like being sick. It is their identity. It does not have to be mine.

I am powerful.

I am not strong because I grew up with privilege and compassion. The solid ground from which I stand was not built from a happy childhood or a trouble-free young life. I have made a million mistakes. I have fought a thousand battles. I know what it's like to have all of your friends look at you with disgust as your life is crumbling before their very eyes. I know the torture of being a slave to substances and I know the absolute war that must be waged against the beast of addictions in order to be free!

My power comes from pain. I beat myself down for years and years. My strength has always been there. But I used against myself. I used it to abuse myself. I have been my own worst abuser. A victim at my own hands. Setting fire to my future. My refusal to accept anything less than supportive people in my life is from all of the years I accepted whatever and whoever came my way.

I don't want to start over anew. I don't want to reinvent myself. I want to continue learning from the very things that once broke me. To grow flowers from graves.

And I found people along the road to my healing that I could trust. People who had been down the same roads I was now embarking upon. See, that is the definition of a healer. Healers do not heal people. Healers are people who have clawed their way out of the darkness themselves; they leave a lighted pathway to show others how to return home to themselves. A healer creates a safe space for the suffering to learn to heal themselves. I found healers. I fought my way back home. And I share my way out to help those people just like me… who think they are buried too deep to get out. Nothing is too horrible, no one is too far gone, and no place is too disgusting for recovery and healing to reach!

I am a healer.

I share every part of myself to inspire hope. To hear and know that there are women who understand. They can stand up and say "me too." It's invaluable. I am willing to share my deepest pain. I will heal out loud. I am part of an evolution in emotional strength. I am proud of how far I have come and I believe it is possible for anyone to grow from the pain they are so afraid to face. I believe in recovery, I believe in the power that comes when women sit together with each other in the dark until the light shines through.

Recovery for me, doesn't mean to become new. I have visited and revisited all the ruins of my life many times. I have searched through the rubble leaving no stone unturned. There is nothing left for me there. All that remains are the things I was never meant to carry; the lessons that were never mine to learn. I have found all the parts that I need to embrace. And I hold them close as I carry them home. They are the building blocks of the life I now live. They are the signs of possibility for the women who are still suffering in their own ghost towns of a past.

I tell the stories of each piece of my life. I share the truth of every invaluable memory of the mistakes of a lost girl in a sea of shame. My story… it's full of twists and turns. Bad decisions and devastating consequences. I have walked through hell and traveled through madness. I tell it all, like it should be told; real and raw and true.

I don't always know what to do or how to feel. Sometimes I get those old feelings of not being enough. Not deserving of the life I have today or the children I have been blessed with. It's okay not to know how to handle everything all at once! Bit by bit, piece by piece we learn that the truths of who we are and the strength to carry on, no matter what, lives in the cracks of our broken hearts. I am guided by all the parts of me that I once believed were too damaged for anyone to ever lay there eyes on.

And there comes a time to burn all that is left behind, down to the ground. Every time I tell my story and own every single word of it, another unneeded piece of that place ignites. And in the middle of all the smoke and flames is a resurrection.

It is not the figure of the broken girl from my childhood. And it's not the animal of my addiction.

Rising from all that has turned to ash…

is the Shape of a woman.

*"When you learn to hold
space for your own story,
you stop telling yourself
to stay quiet.
You stop caring
what the neighbors will think.
You strike with lightening.
With a charge of justice,
and empower others to speak
because your story is hers,
and her healing is ours."*

-Tanya Markul

The Call To Arms

I am recovering from many things. Each one shadowing the other to create my once very dark and destitute world. But each play an irreplaceable part in my strength as a woman today. I have spun shit into gold. Turned hell into hope. There is an army of women inside of me that will not lie down to the injustices we impose onto ourselves.

I stand with me.

I stand with you.

Together we can stand in honor and redemption. Being unloved has taught me how to love with incredible fierceness. All the years of remaining silent has gifted me a thundering voice. Crawling the streets of addiction gave me an unshakable belief in recovery!

Spending years behind bars empowered a woman who fights for her freedom. Coming so close to death has left me fully alive!

I have recycled my pain into pure wildfire.

This collective silencing of the things that burn inside us only fuels the fires of destructive habits. Nothing is gained by remaining on our knees begging for validation. Healing out loud does not make you intolerable! Speaking of the things that hurt your life does not make you unbearable to be around. Bringing people to answer to their behaviors does not make you a traitor. And owning up to the mistakes of your life does not make you unlovable.

I grieve with all women. Their pain is my pain. My healing is their healing. When one woman heals her life… and heals out loud and unrestricted… it touches all the women around her. Our healing makes possible for our daughters to walk barefoot in the soil… free flowing and in their own stories. And until every single woman is free from her shackles I will fight. I will fight for fierce femininity, I will bring forth the nurturer inside of me and courageously remain tender. There is nothing weak in womanhood.

There is incredible power in sisterhood. Let's sit together and change the world.

One wounded woman at a time.

Please feel free to follow me or contact me on Instagram @ Resurrektion_of_me

I am here for you.

Manifesto Of The Brave And Broken-Hearted

"There is no greater threat to the critics
and cynics and fear-mongers
than those of us who are willing to fall
because we have learned how to rise.

With skinned knees and bruised hearts;
we choose owning our stories of struggle,

over hiding, over hustling, over pretending.

When we deny our stories, they define us.
When we run from struggle, we are never free.
So we turn toward truth and look it in the eye.

We will not be characters in our stories.
Not villains, not victims, not even heroes.
We are the authors of our lives.
We write our own daring endings.

We craft love from heartbreak,
compassion from shame,
grace from disappointment,
courage from failure.

Showing up is our power.
Our story is our way home. Truth is our song.
We are the brave and broken-hearted.
We are rising strong."

-Brene Brown

I Used To Try To Be Good

"I thought no one wanted me as I was, so Good was my go-to.

But Good got me nowhere. Not like Truth.

Truth, she tore me to shreds, devoured me whole and spit me out shaking and new.

Truth keeps a box of matches in my pocket.

While Good, made me afraid of transformative fire.

Truth keeps me real, even if it makes everyone in the room uncomfortable.

And Truth, unlike Good, doesn't let me bow down to bullshit or soap boxes.

Truth doesn't let me give in to bullies, misguided and fear based criticism or cowards.

Truth is a queen and a humanitarian, while Good, she's a silent scared little sheep.

Truth knows that Good dulls my already radiant, fierce and loving soul.

Good showed me how to hide my wings, my words, and angel vision.

Truth taught me to be brave.

Truth taught me how to respect myself.

Truth allows me to hold me hold impenetrable space for any story, but first and foremost, for my own.

And Truth, well, she changes everything, and friend, she's coming for you too."

-Tanya Markul

Made in the USA
Columbia, SC
15 February 2019